CIVIC CENTER

How Do Hybrid
Cars Work?

by Richard Hantula

**Science and Curriculum Consultant: Debra Voege, M.A.,
Science Curriculum Resource Teacher**

CHELSEA
CLUBHOUSE
An Imprint of Chelsea House Publishers

Science in the Real World: How Do Hybrid Cars Work?

Copyright © 2010 by Infobase Publishing

Chelsea Clubhouse
An imprint of Chelsea House Publishers
132 West 31st Street
New York NY 10001

Library of Congress Cataloging-in-Publication Data
Hantula, Richard.
        How do hybrid cars work? / by Richard Hantula; science and curriculum consultant, Debra Voege.
            p. cm. — (Science in the real world)
        Includes bibliographical references and index.
        ISBN 978-1-60413-476-6
        1. Hybrid electric cars—Juvenile literature. I. Voege, Debra. II. Title. III. Series.
    TL221.15.H36 2010
    629.22'93—dc22   2009012509

Chelsea Clubhouse books are available at special discounts when purchased in bulk quantities for businesses, associations, institutions, or sales promotions. Please call our Special Sales Department in New York at (212) 967-8800 or (800) 322-8755.

You can find Chelsea Clubhouse on the World Wide Web at http://www.chelseahouse.com

Developed for Chelsea House by RJF Publishing LLC (www.RJFpublishing.com)
Text and cover design by Tammy West/Westgraphix LLC
Illustrations by Spectrum Creative Inc.
Photo research by Edward A. Thomas
Index by Nila Glikin

Photo Credits: 4, 5, 21: iStockphoto; 8: Nancy Honey/Photolibrary; 9, 12, 16, 18, 19, 26: AP/Wide World Photos; 13: Car Culture (Getty Images); 14: Dr. Ing. h.c. F. Porsche AG, Historical Archive; 15: dpa/Landov; 17: © Frances Roberts/Alamy; 22: Getty Images; 24: Mark Elias/Bloomberg News/Landov; 25: © Car Culture/Corbis; 28: © GIPhotoStockZ/Alamy.

Printed and bound in the United States of America

Bang RJF 10 9 8 7 6 5 4 3 2 1

Table of Contents

Words that are defined in the Glossary are in **bold** type
the first time they appear in the text.

Saving on Gas, Saving the Air

Cars have been around for more than 100 years. They have changed a lot in that time. Today's cars are faster and more reliable than those of long ago. They are also safer and more comfortable.

One thing has not changed: the way most cars work. Most cars of the past ran on fuel made from oil. That's still true today. Usually the fuel is gasoline (often called "gas"for short). Sometimes it is **diesel fuel**. Both come from oil.

A driver fills his car's tank with gasoline, a fuel that is made from oil.

The Trouble with Oil

Oil is a very good source of energy, but using it has problems. One problem is that oil is not a **renewable resource**. Once it's used, it's gone. If people keep on using it, eventually the world will run out of oil. Meanwhile, as oil gets less plentiful, fuels made from it will probably get more and more costly over time.

Another problem is that using fuels made from oil releases certain gases into the air. Some of these gases can be bad for people's health. Many scientists say that some of the gases are changing Earth's climate.

These are serious problems because the world has a huge number of **vehicles**, and every year more are produced. In 2007, for example, more than 50 million cars were made. If you include trucks and buses, the number of new vehicles made that year gets even bigger.

One way to deal with these problems is to use less oil. This is where hybrid cars come in. They get their power from electricity as well as from gasoline (or diesel). As a result, they use less gas.

There are many millions of cars, trucks, and buses on the roads in the United States and around the world.

DID YOU KNOW ?

What Is a "Hybrid"?

Any vehicle that has two sources of power can be called a hybrid. A **moped** is a hybrid. It has an engine, but you can also make it go by pedaling. When people talk about hybrid cars, they usually mean a car that has both a gasoline engine and an **electric motor**.

Gasoline Cars

The drawbacks of traditional cars bother a lot of people. Still, traditional cars have many good points. With a full tank of gas, they can go hundreds of miles. When it's time to refill the gas tank, refueling is easy to do. Gas stations are nearly everywhere, and refueling takes just a few minutes.

Also, modern gasoline engines provide a lot of power. They make it easy to drive at highway speeds and also to pass other cars safely when necessary.

Most gasoline car engines have four, six, or eight cylinders. In each cylinder, there's a piston that moves up and down as shown here.

How a Typical Gasoline Engine Works

1 A mixture of gasoline and air goes into the cylinder

Spark Plug

Intake Valve

Exhaust Valve

Cylinder

Piston

Crankshaft

2 The piston moves up, squeezing the gasoline-air mixture, and a spark makes the gasoline and air explode

3 The explosion pushes the piston down and turns the crankshaft

4 The piston moves up again and pushes out the burned gasoline-air mixture so the cycle can start again

Internal-Combustion Engine

Traditional cars use an **internal-combustion engine**. This means the fuel is burned, or combusted, inside the engine. The combustion takes place inside a hollow part of the engine called a cylinder. Another part, called a piston, can move up and down in the cylinder. When the engine runs, gasoline and air are put in the cylinder, and a spark is created. This results in very fast combustion—an explosion— that pushes the piston down. The piston is connected to a crankshaft. This shaft converts the up-and-down movement of the piston into a turning motion, which can be used to turn the car's wheels.

The turning of the crankshaft also causes the piston to rise back up in the cylinder. At the right moment, another explosion occurs in the cylinder, pushing the piston back down. The constant series of explosions keeps the crankshaft turning. A typical car has several cylinders. All of them help to turn the crankshaft.

Making Internal Combustion Possible

Besides the engine, a car needs certain other basic things for internal combustion to take place. These things include a fuel tank, for storing gasoline, and a **battery**, which supplies the electricity to make the sparks.

Electric Cars

The first electric cars were made in the 19th century. A few are still made today. Instead of a gas tank, they usually have batteries, which store electricity. Instead of an internal-combustion engine, they have an electric motor. The motor uses electricity from the batteries to produce a turning action. This action is used to turn the car's wheels.

Electric cars have some strong points. They are quiet and clean. Because they run on electricity, they cause little or no **pollution**.

This woman has found a recharging station for her electric car, but these stations are not common.

Drawbacks

Electric cars have never really caught on, though. One problem is the batteries. They're heavy, and they take up a lot of space. Also, until recently the batteries haven't been able to hold enough energy to let an electric car go as far or as fast as traditional cars can.

Some car companies made a small number of electric

cars and pickup trucks in the 1990s. The cars had a top speed of around 80 miles (130 kilometers) an hour. They couldn't go much farther than 100 miles (160 kilometers) before the batteries had to be recharged.

Recharging the batteries takes a lot of time. Usually you have to find a way to plug the car into the public power system. If you can't recharge at home, finding a place to recharge can be hard. Recharging stations are few and far between. Recent advances in batteries have made the situation a little better. Still, electric cars are rare in the United States.

DID YOU KNOW **?**

Tesla's Roadster

Better electric cars are on the way. In 2008, one car company made an electric sports car. Called the Tesla Roadster (see photo above), this car had a top speed of 125 miles (200 kilometers) per hour and could travel about 220 miles (350 kilometers) on one charge. Tesla was also working on an electric car that could hold five people and travel up to 300 miles (480 kilometers) between charges. It was expected to be more expensive than most cars, though.

Inside a Hybrid

A hybrid car gets power from both a gasoline engine and an electric motor. The engine and motor can work together in different ways. In some hybrids there are times when only one of them operates.

In hybrid cars, the engine can automatically shut off when it is not needed—for example, at a red light or in stop-and-go traffic. This is one reason why hybrids usually use less gasoline than traditional cars. Another reason is that since the electric motor does some of the work of moving the car, the

In a parallel hybrid, both the engine and the electric motor make the wheels turn. In a series hybrid, the motor turns the wheels, while the engine runs a generator to make electricity.

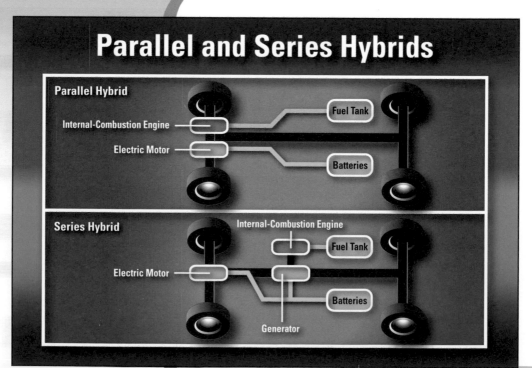

Parallel and Series Hybrids

Parallel Hybrid
Internal-Combustion Engine
Electric Motor
Fuel Tank
Batteries

Series Hybrid
Internal-Combustion Engine
Electric Motor
Fuel Tank
Batteries
Generator

gasoline engine is usually smaller than in traditional cars.

The motor—as in electric cars—gets power from large batteries. Unlike ordinary electric cars, most of today's hybrids don't need to be plugged in to get recharged. Instead, their batteries can be recharged while the car is being used. The car may have a **generator** to make electricity. This generator is powered by the gasoline engine. In some hybrids the electric motor itself works as a generator at times.

Design Types

There are two basic ways the engine and motor can work together. They are called parallel and series. In a parallel hybrid, the engine and motor both supply power that drives the wheels. In a series hybrid, the gasoline engine is used to generate electricity; the electric motor drives the wheels.

DID YOU KNOW?

Mild and Full

Some hybrids are called **mild hybrids**. Others are called **full hybrids**. The difference has to do with the electric motor. If the motor can drive the car by itself, without the gasoline engine, then the car is a full hybrid. The Ford Escape Hybrid is one example of a car that can do this. If the electric motor ordinarily just assists the engine, the car is a mild hybrid. Honda's hybrid Civic is an example of a mild hybrid.

Hybrids on the Road

A hybrid is a cross between two types of cars. It takes some features from gasoline cars. It also takes some from electric cars. This lets it improve on some of the weak points of each type.

Hybrids can go farther than electric cars. Their top speed tends to be higher. Unlike electric cars, they generally don't need to be plugged in for a recharge.

A hybrid car's electric motor gives it good power for going uphill or passing. Hybrids tend to be quieter than traditional gasoline cars. Since a hybrid's internal-combustion engine generally doesn't burn as much fuel, hybrids use up less of the world's oil and cause less pollution.

The dashboard of a hybrid car may display information about how the engine and motor are working together and how much charge the battery has.

Saving on Gasoline

There are several reasons why a hybrid usually uses less gasoline than a similar car with a traditional engine. It doesn't have to use fuel for idling, since the engine can just shut off when the car is stopped. Also, since the electric motor helps power the car, the engine doesn't need to be as big and heavy as in a traditional car. Smaller gasoline engines tend to be more efficient than large ones, and they burn less fuel. More savings come if the electric motor can drive the car at low speeds all by itself. Gasoline engines are not very efficient at low speeds.

Some hybrid cars are started by pushing a Power button.

DID YOU KNOW ?

Slowdown Energy

Many hybrids use a special trick to avoid wasting energy. When a car slows down by braking, the energy of the wheels has to go somewhere. In traditional cars it turns into heat in the brakes. In other words, it goes to waste. Many hybrid (and electric) cars put much of this energy to good use. They capture the energy and send it to the motor, which then works as a generator and makes electricity. The electricity can be stored in the batteries, ready for later use. This useful way of making electricity from the energy of the wheels is called regenerative braking.

Hybrid History

It's hard to say who made the first hybrid. Having two different power sources is actually an old idea.

The first important hybrid that we know of today was made around 1900 by the famous Austrian car designer Ferdinand Porsche. The car had a gasoline engine, and there were electric motors in the wheel hubs. It was a series hybrid. The engine ran a generator that made electricity.

Other people also made hybrids in the early 20th century. But the internal-combustion car became very popular. It was powerful, and fuel was cheap and easy to get. Also, hybrid cars cost more to make. For decades few people bothered to even experiment with them.

This photo shows Ferdinand Porsche's first hybrid car.

A Hybrid Boom

Toward the end of the 20th century the situation changed. Gasoline started to get more costly. At the same time, people began to realize that the world's oil might someday be all used up. Meanwhile, more and more people worried about the pollution caused by burning fuels made from oil. Finally, two big Japanese car companies introduced hybrid cars.

Toyota started selling the Prius in Japan in 1997. Honda introduced the Insight in 1999. The Insight had very good gas mileage. It was just a small two-seater, however, and did not sell well. The Prius was a midsize car. It proved popular. Toyota, Honda, and other companies soon began to introduce new hybrid models of midsize or larger cars.

DID YOU KNOW ?

Ferdinand Porsche

Ferdinand Porsche was one of greatest car engineers of all time. He was born in 1875 in what is now the Czech Republic (a country in Europe). Around 1900, while working for the Lohner company, he made the first well-known hybrid car. He later started his own company. He led the team of designers and engineers that created the famous Volkswagen "Beetle." (The photo above shows a 1939 model.) Porsche died in 1951.

More and More Hybrids

The Prius was first sold in the United States in 2000. Seven years later it became the first hybrid to rank among the top-ten best-selling cars in the United States. Toyota brought out hybrid versions of its Highlander and Lexus sport-utility vehicles (SUVs) in 2005. In 2006, Toyota came out with hybrid versions of its popular Camry and Lexus sedans. By spring 2007 the company had sold more than 1 million hybrids around the world. A year later, total sales of the Prius alone passed 1 million.

Honda stopped making its original Insight in 2006. It had more success with a hybrid version of its very popular Civic. This hybrid, launched in 2003, was about the size of the Prius.

Hybrids now come in all sizes, from small and midsize cars to SUVs such as this one.

In 2009, Honda came out with a new, slightly larger version of the Insight.

In 2004, Ford brought out the first hybrid made by a U.S. company. The car was a hybrid version of the Escape SUV. It was actually the first hybrid SUV in the world. In the following years, hybrid versions of other makes of cars also came on the market.

This taxi is a hybrid. Since taxis may be on the road all day long, hybrid models can save a lot of gasoline.

U.S. Sales Grow

Hybrids became available in the United States a few years later than in Japan. Today, the number of hybrid models on the U.S. market is still far smaller than the number of traditional car models. Even so, more and more Americans are buying hybrids. In 2007, they bought more than 350,000 new hybrid vehicles. This was 38 percent more than in 2006.

DID YOU KNOW ?

Power-Assist Hybrids

Certain hybrids are sometimes called power-assist hybrids. Usually these are mild hybrids. The electric motor helps the engine at times—such as when accelerating. Honda's Civic hybrid is an example.

Not Just Cars

There are also hybrid trucks and buses on the road today. In some of them, the engine runs on gasoline. In others, it runs on diesel fuel. In addition, there are vehicles in which the engine uses a **turbine** instead of the traditional cylinders with pistons. Whatever the type of engine, the reasons for using a hybrid design are much the same as for cars. Hybrid buses and trucks tend to use less fuel and create less pollution than traditional buses and trucks.

Many cities now use hybrid buses to save fuel and keep the air cleaner.

Dual-Mode Trucks and Buses

Some makers of hybrid cars use the name "dual mode" for their design. This name is also often used in a different way. It refers to trucks and buses that have two different power sources but are not really hybrids. The two power sources work independently. In hybrids, the two power sources generally work together. In dual-mode vehicles, they are used at different times, in different situations. For example, the Silver Line in Boston, Massachusetts, has dual-mode buses. For part of their route they use an electric motor powered by an overhead line. For other parts they use a diesel engine.

This truck, owned by a Vermont power company, uses less than half the fuel that the company's traditional trucks use.

Saving the Environment

Oil is a major cause of pollution. The same is true of the fuels made from it. For one thing, oil is sometimes accidentally spilled into the environment. This can harm plants and wildlife. Another problem arises when oil is refined, or made, into fuels. This process releases pollutants into the environment. Still another problem occurs when fuels such as gasoline are used. Burning them puts pollutants into the air. In fact, the U.S. Environmental Protection Agency (EPA) says that driving a car "is probably a typical citizen's most 'polluting' daily activity."

Cars put various substances into the air. One of them is carbon monoxide. This gas can cause health problems. Other gases called nitrogen oxides can lead to **smog**, which can also be harmful to people's health. Substances called hydrocarbons are another potential cause of smog. Cars also produce large amounts of so-called greenhouse gases, such as

carbon dioxide. Many scientists think that greenhouse gases in the air are making the world's climate warmer. This climate change is known as **global warming**.

Gases that go into the air when gasoline is burned can be a major cause of air pollution.

Grading Cars for Pollution

Like traditional cars, hybrids burn fuel. They generally use less, however, and so they cause less pollution. For this reason, hybrids usually score well when the EPA grades cars on their environmental effects. The grades range from 0 to 10, where 10 means best, or cleanest. For example, the 2009 Nissan Altima Hybrid, a midsize car, scored 9 for greenhouse gas and 9.5 for air pollution. By contrast, the 2009 Lexus SC430, a small non-hybrid from Toyota, scored only 5 for greenhouse gas and got similarly low marks for air pollution.

DID YOU KNOW ?

Pollution Limits

In the United States there are laws that put limits on certain pollutants from cars. One of them is the Clean Air Act of 1970. Another is the Clean Air Act of 1990, which made refineries produce gasoline that burns more cleanly. States such as California also have limits on certain pollutants.

Saving Fuel

Using less fuel can help the environment. Many people would like to use less for another reason as well. Gasoline costs money, and the price tends to keep going up. Sometimes it does go down. But over the long term, the price tends to gradually go up.

A common way of telling how well, or efficiently, a car uses gasoline is to look at its fuel economy. This is the number of miles it can go on 1 gallon. (A mile is about 1.6 kilometers.) Partly this depends on how the car gets its power. Hybrids can use less gasoline because they get some of their power from electricity. Mileage per gallon also depends on the car's weight. It takes more energy to move

Hybrids, such as this one being driven in New York City, usually use less gasoline in city than in highway driving.

a heavy car than a light one. The shape of the car is another factor. A moving car pushes against the air, and this takes energy. Some shapes have less "drag." They slip through the air more easily than others. Factors like these explain why different cars—even different hybrids—don't all get the same number of miles per gallon.

Grading Cars for Fuel Use

If you want to compare different cars, mileage figures from the EPA can help. The agency measures all cars the same way. It found that the 2009 Toyota Prius could do 48 miles per gallon (20 kilometers per liter) in city driving and 45 miles per gallon (19 kilometers per liter) on the highway. Traditional cars usually get better mileage on the highway than in the city. The Prius does better in the city because it uses its electric motor more there.

DID YOU KNOW ?

Mileage Standards

In the United States the average fuel usage of new cars has to be better than a certain level. A 2007 law said this level will rise to 35 miles per gallon (14.9 kilometers per liter) by the year 2020.

Some Drawbacks of Hybrids

Hybrids have some disadvantages. For one thing, they tend to cost more to buy than similar traditional cars. Of course, they do save money for their owners by using less gasoline.

Hybrids are often smaller and less powerful than similar non-hybrid cars. This can be a drawback for people who like big, powerful cars. Some hybrids do have big engines. These "muscle" hybrids can deliver a lot of power, but they don't save much on gasoline. The hybrid version of Toyota's 2009 Highlander SUV got just 25 miles per gallon (10.6 kilometers per liter) on the highway, according to the EPA. The non-hybrid

Some hybrids, such as this one, have more power but don't save as much on gasoline.

version was almost as good, averaging 23 to 24 miles per gallon (9. 8 to 10.2 kilometers per liter).

batteries

Expensive Batteries and Service

The batteries in a hybrid are heavy. Their weight increases the amount of energy needed to make the car go. Also, they take up a lot of space. They make the car less roomy. In addition, they are very expensive. They are very reliable and should last a long time, but if hybrid batteries ever need to be replaced, the cost will be high.

Hybrids are complicated cars. Fewer service people know how to fix them. Repairs may sometimes cost more than for traditional cars. But this situation may change as more and more hybrids appear on the road.

Car makers are trying to make the batteries in hybrids smaller and lighter. This model has smaller-than-usual batteries.

DID YOU KNOW ?

Lowering the Cost

Various programs intended to boost hybrid use can help lower the cost of hybrid cars. Some hybrid buyers get savings on taxes. Hybrid owners may pay less for insurance. In some areas, hybrid drivers can park for free or at a reduced rate.

Plug-Ins

Almost all hybrids save on gasoline use. Some save more. Some less. One way a hybrid could get even better fuel economy would be to borrow a feature of electric cars, which usually get their electricity by being plugged into the power grid.

A hybrid that could plug in could save in a couple of ways. Some of the fuel used by hybrids goes to make electricity. A hybrid would use less gasoline if its batteries could be charged at home or at a charging station. Also, it might be able to do a lot of short trips without using its gasoline engine at all. With really good batteries, a plug-in hybrid might be

This experimental model of a plug-in hybrid is getting more energy for its batteries at a charging station.

able to go long distances on electric power. Such a plug-in might use its engine only if it needed to generate more electricity.

As of early 2009, there already were some plug-in hybrids on the road. People made them by converting regular hybrids they had bought. Some car companies said they would soon start selling plug-in hybrids.

Two-Way Connection

There is another way plug-in hybrids might save money and lower pollution. Hybrids make electricity both with their engine and with regenerative braking. Any electricity they don't use gets stored in their batteries. Some-day it may be practical for them to feed extra electricity to the public power grid when they are plugged in. Hybrid owners could be paid for the electricity they provide to the power company. An added benefit of this type of plug-in is that it would help the power grid have a steady supply of electricity.

More Options

Gasoline is the most common fuel used today in hybrid cars. Car companies are looking at other fuels for possible use. A good alternative fuel might cost less, cut pollution more, or be better at reducing the overall use of oil.

Alternative fuels are already used in some traditional cars, buses, or trucks. One alternative fuel is **ethanol**. Another is natural gas. Yet another is liquefied petroleum gas (propane), often called LPG for short. In some countries, LPG is cheaper than gasoline. The Hyundai company planned to start selling an LPG hybrid in 2009 in South Korea. Car companies are also studying the

The experimental car and bus shown here, parked outside the California Science Center in Los Angeles, both run on hydrogen.

use of a so-called flex-fuel engine in hybrids. Flex-fuel engines are flexible. They can run on more than one kind of fuel.

In addition, car companies are looking into the use of **fuel cells** in hybrids. Fuel cells use hydrogen to make electricity. The only thing they give off in the process is water! Toyota's experimental FCHV (Fuel-Cell Hybrid Vehicle) has a fuel cell instead of an internal-combustion engine. One problem with fuel cells is that right now hydrogen is not widely available. Another problem is that fuel cells so far tend to cost a lot.

Government Backing

The U.S. government supports research on hybrid cars. A 2007 law provided money for work on plug-in hybrids and on better batteries. It even called for a college contest to develop plug-ins. It also encouraged the use of hybrids by the government. This kind of support for hybrid cars may well increase over the coming years.

DID YOU KNOW ?

Tribrids

Every power source has strong points and weak points. Finding the best combination for hybrids is a tough job. Someday there may even be "tribrid" vehicles—hybrids that use three different power sources.

Glossary

battery—A device that stores electricity.

carbon dioxide—One of the gases produced by burning fuels like gasoline.

diesel fuel—A type of fuel made from oil. It is commonly used in large **vehicles** such as trucks and locomotives. Some cars use it.

electric motor—A machine that uses electricity to produce a turning action. This action can turn the wheels of a car.

ethanol—A type of alcohol often used as a fuel. It is usually made from plants or from oil.

fuel cell—A device that uses a reaction between two substances to make electricity. Usually one of the substances is hydrogen.

full hybrid—A hybrid car in which the **electric motor** can drive the wheels by itself.

generator—A machine that uses a turning action to produce electricity.

global warming—A gradual warming of Earth's climate. Many scientists think that the burning of fuels like gasoline helps cause it.

internal-combustion engine—An engine that burns fuel inside itself in order to produce power.

mild hybrid—A hybrid car in which the **electric motor** usually just assists the **internal-combustion engine**.

moped—A small motorbike with pedals, which can be used along with the engine to make the bike go. The name comes from "*mot*or" and "*ped*al."

pollution—Harmful or dangerous substances that are put into the environment.

renewable resource—A resource, such as a source of energy, that never gets used up. Energy sources such as sunlight and wind are renewable.

smog—A type of air **pollution** found in some big cities. One cause is the burning of fuel by cars. The word comes from "*sm*oke" and "f*og*."

turbine—A machine with a turning action that can make electricity or power **vehicle** wheels.

vehicle—Something that carries people and things around. Cars, buses, and trucks are examples of vehicles.

To Learn More

Read these books:

Flammang, James M. *Cars*. Ann Arbor, Mich.: Cherry Lake, 2009.

Hammond, Richard. *Car Science*. New York: Dorling Kindersley, 2008.

Povey, Karen D. *Energy Alternatives*. Detroit: Lucent, 2007.

Look up these Web sites:

Department of Energy, Office of Energy Efficiency and Renewable Energy
http://www.afdc.energy.gov/afdc/vehicles/hybrid_electric.html

How Stuff Works
http://www.howstuffworks.com/hybrid-car.htm

HybridCars.com
http://www.hybridcars.com

Toyota Children's Question Room
http://www.toyota.co.jp/en/kids/faq/j/05

Union of Concerned Scientists
http://www.hybridcenter.org/hybrid-center-how-hybrid-cars-work-under-the-hood.html

Key Internet search terms:

automobile, battery, car, electric motor, gasoline, hybrid car, internal combustion, plug-in

Index

About the Author

Richard Hantula has written, edited, and translated books and articles on science and technology for more than three decades. He was the senior U.S. editor for the *Macmillan Encyclopedia of Science*.